Dedicated to
my beautiful family

Be careful for nothing; but in every thing
by prayer and supplication with thanksgiving
let your requests be made known to God.

And the peace of God, which passeth all understanding,
shall keep your hearts and minds through Jesus Christ.

Philippians 4:6

For: _______________
From: _______________

I am blessed to be a mother.
I pray for my child each day.
I bow my head,
lift my hands in prayer,
and this is what I say.

Heavenly Father,
Please surround my child with
protection. Help my child feel
secure. Keep my child safe.

Empower my child with courage,
knowing you are always there to
guide each step and prepare the way.

Comfort my child with your
presence should any fear or worry
enter heart or mind.

With your divine protection,
keep away anything
hurtful or unkind.

Guard my child's mind
from worry and negative influences
that seek to steal peace.

Keep your mighty shield of
protection around my child and
grant serenity please.

Help my child be brave in the face
of challenges and stay strong
through the ups and downs of life.

Give my child strength
in body and spirit to persevere
through any hardship and strife.

Help my child stand strong
in difficult times and see troubles as
opportunities to know You deeply.

Help my child face obstacles
with fortitude and courage,
and trust You completely.

Give my child a positive
outlook and an unshakeable
faith in You.

Grant my child hope
in all circumstances,
a reminder of Your love so true.

Dear Father,
Please bless and keep my child
healthy, flourishing and well.

Nourish my child's body, mind
and spirit and let my child enjoy
prosperity and good health.

Help my child develop
healthy habits that foster growth
and promote well-being.

When my child feels
weak or unwell, please
provide strength and healing.

If my child ever feels
cold or ill, please restore
good health and warmth.

Touch my child with your
healing hands and safeguard
my child from harm.

Please help my child know
and care for the body as the
temple of Your spirit.

May my child walk in Your
light and love and
feel confident in it.

Guide my child to seek Your
lasting peace and a sense of
contentment so deep.

Fill my child with purpose
and uplifting dreams and
bless with tranquil sleep.

Surround my child with
good influences, people
true, honest and kind.

Build relationships that
support growth in faith and
encourage doing what is right.

Bless my child with kindness
and compassion to treat others
and live with dignity.

May my child humbly
ask forgiveness when needed
and forgive others sincerely.

Give my child a calm and
gentle spirit to treat others and self
with respect, patience and love.

Please let my child's thoughts,
words and actions reflect
Your goodness from above.

Protect my child from
deception and injury
from anything and anyone.

Help my child resist
temptation and follow
the teachings of Your Son.

Direct my child's steps,
Dear Lord. Grant my child
wisdom beyond years.

Guide my child's thoughts,
choices and actions to put
faith over fear.

Grant my child a passion
for learning. Help my child
grow in understanding and faith.

Give my child discipline
to avoid evil and
discernment to stay safe.

Please bless my child with gifts
and talents to fill the world
with hope and light.

May my child be grateful for
every blessing and always find
favor in your sight.

Please let love and joy overflow
in my child's life. Guard my child's
heart from sorrow and despair.

I pray for happiness, success,
and contentment for my child
under Your care.

May the Bible serve as a guiding
source and help my child become the
person You created this child to be.

Fill my child's mind, body
and spirit with a desire
to know truth and live free.

I pray my child will always
seek your guidance and
You will see my child through.

May my child use gifts
for Your glory and experience the
joy of fellowship with You.

Please pour forth your blessings
upon my child, love, light,
peace, strength and grace.

Thank You, Heavenly Father.
I pray your loving arms
will hold my child always.

In
Jesus'
glorious
name,

AMEN

Note